Your Transformative Journey

Making the Conscious Decision to Explore Your Unconscious Self

Mini-Guide No: YOU101

Discover Other Titles by Deb Donnell

Christchurch, NZ
"Then and Now" Series

Responders (with Pete Seager)

Café Reflections: Christchurch City

Trails to Treasure

Creating Published Diamonds

Your Transformative Journey

Making the Conscious Decision to Explore Your Unconscious Self

Deb Donnell

Mini-Guide No: YOU101

This Mini-Guide is part of the YOU Series.

Published by
Keswin Publishing Ltd
P O Box 36-476, Merivale
Christchurch 8146. New Zealand
Tel: +64 3 421 7834
Email: keswinpublishing@keswingroup.com
Website: https://keswinpublishing.com

Your Transformative Journey - YOU101

Edition ISBNs:
PDF: 978-0-9582780-4-1
Ebook (Lulu): 978-0-9582780-5-8
Ebook (Smashwords): 978-0-9582780-8-9
Print: 978-0-9582780-7-2

A catalogue of this book is available from the National Library of New Zealand.

"Transformation is a process, and as life happens there are tons of ups and downs. It's a journey of discovery—there are moments on mountaintops and moments in deep valleys of despair."

—Rick Warren

Contents

Warning—Disclaimer

The Transformative Journey is not easy. The decisions you make and the actions you take to change your life for the better are uniquely yours. What has worked for the author may not work for you. It's important to note that there is no quick-fix or fast-track process for personal development. It is only through **your commitment** to the Transformative Journey, and **your continued efforts and persistence** to keep applying the information and resources shared within this book to your life, that you will achieve the outcome you desire. It is also recommended that you study a wide variety of material on the subject, in order to make informed decisions and take the actions that are appropriate and ecological for you.

Therefore, this book is sold with the understanding that the author and publisher are not engaged by you to render any type of psychological, legal, financial, or any other kind of professional advice. The purpose of this book is to inform, educate and entertain. Neither the publisher nor the author shall be liable for any physical, psychological, emotional, financial, or commercial damages, including, but not limited to, special, incidental, consequential or other damages.

The author and publisher's views and rights are the same. **You take full ownership of, and are fully responsible and accountable for your own choices, actions, and results. If you do not agree to be bound by these terms, please return this book to the publisher or distributor for a full refund.**

Introduction

"I'm not a teacher: only a fellow-traveler of whom you asked the way. I pointed ahead—ahead of myself as well as you."

—George Bernard Shaw

Welcome, fellow traveller. I do not know what has led you here, to study your Transformative Journey, but I feel very privileged to be chosen as your guide. Please read the George Bernard Shaw quote at the start of this chapter, as it's important for you to realise that I don't have the answers to your Quest. Only you know what is meaningful for you.

My role in your Journey is to provide you with the tools and resources that I've found effective on my own adventures, and believe you may find effective too. This KESWIN™ mini-guide is the first in the 'YOU' series, focusing on personal development. It provides an overview of what you can expect on your Transformative Journey.

I have based this overview on the work of Joseph Campbell. He studied the world's mythologies and religions, and found commonalities of the archetypal Hero's Journey. His many publications included *The Hero of a Thousand Faces.*

I followed up my reading of his book with Christopher Vogler's *The Writer's Journey—Mythic Structure for Writers.* Also based on

Joseph Campbell's book, it gave me pause to reflect on my own Transformative Journeys, as well as ones of other people that I know, follow, or have studied.

At the same time as studying these two books, I worked towards my NS-NLP Master Practitioner Certification.

NS (Neuro-Semantics) and NLP (Neuro-Linguistics Programming) are two very powerful tools for self-management. They empower people to run their own brain, as well as control and change the narratives and mind-movies of their lives.

It became crystal clear to me how these powerful resources all fitted together, and how, having travelled ahead of you, I could bring back and share the gems I discovered.

In June and July 2018, the world experienced one of the most gripping real life dramas with all the elements of the Heroic Quest story.

Members of the Wild Boars Soccer Team were trapped in Thailand's Tham Luang cave, 4 kilometres (2.5 miles) deep inside the belly of the Earth.

On 23 June 2018, twelve boys (aged 11–17) and their 25 year old coach had gone into the cave. They didn't return home that day. The authorities were alerted. For 9 days their fate was unknown. Experienced cave divers searched the cave system, swimming in cold, dark, murky waters. When two British divers found all 13 still alive on 2 July 2018, the news went viral over the Internet.

The eleven hour return journey to the team was extremely challenging for experienced cave divers. There were long stretches (up to 40 minutes) of diving through murky water with low visibility. One very narrow and steep part required the divers to remove their tanks in order to squeeze through the dangerous gap.

How would the 12 boys and their coach, weakened from nine days of no food, and no diving experience, be able to make this dangerous journey out of the cave safely?

Multiple options were discussed by the rescuers. Over ten thousand people worked together as one Hero to achieve "mission impossible".

Sadly, a life was lost on 6 July 2018. A former Thai Navy Seal diver, Saman Kunan, ran out of oxygen during one of his missions to lay reserve oxygen tanks along the route. His sacrifice meant the rescue plan had to be revised. The rescuers' resolve strengthened to succeed at bringing the 12 boys and their coach safely out.

Rescuers had been working around the clock to lower the water level in the cave system, and reduce the return journey time for the divers. Monsoon rains were forecast, which increased the risk to the team, who were trapped on a small rocky ledge. In addition, the oxygen supply was running low—another life-threatening challenge.

The evacuation of the team couldn't wait. Over the course of three days (8, 9 and 10 July 2018), each survivor was bought out by two assigned divers, supported by 90 more along the route, with hundreds forming a daisy chain in the unflooded parts of the cave.

Like the rest of the world, I cheered when each boy was safely brought out, and anxiously worried about the ones remaining inside. Miraculously, all thirteen were safely evacuated.

"Mission complete" was declared. The team spent a week quarantined in a hospital to recover. Read the full story of the search and rescue:
https://en.wikipedia.org/wiki/Tham_Luang_cave_rescue

Over the years, I have been on many Transformative Journeys of my own, though none as dangerous or dramatic as the Wild Boars' rescue. I have also guided others on theirs. Continuous self-improvement and growth is a foundation of my life, in the books I write and publish, and in the training and mentoring I provide.

I've carried George Bernard Shaw's quote with me since 1999. I knew I was pointing the way ahead of myself, as much as anyone else.

In 2003, I had a vision of creating a learning and networking centre that empowered individuals to build independent businesses with the support and encouragement of like-minded people. This was in the early days of the Internet, when the price of developing a platform like this was prohibitive.

The Quest I set myself almost overwhelmed me. Rather than refuse the Call to the Journey, I realised that the only way to achieve my vision was to chunk it down into mini excursions.

Some of these excursions have moved me forward on the path. Others have shunted me onto detours which, at first, seemed to take me in the opposite direction to where I wanted to go.

My mini-excursions have developed my talents and attributes (which I also refer to as my KESWIN™), so that I my 2003 vision is now a reality. I have developed the resources to build my learning and networking centre, and guide others to avoid pitfalls, obstacles and challenges.

I enjoy creating acronyms. The word KESWIN™ is formed from the initials of words that describe the different stages of a hero's Transformative Journey:

Knowledge
Experiences
Skill-sets
Wisdom
Ideas
Narratives

This mini-guide provides you with an overview of what you can expect on your Transformative Journey. As you set off into the unknown, I imagine that there will be some degree of fear. I'm sure that you've heard many acronyms for the word FEAR. My favourite one is *Feeling Excited And Ready*, and I am feeling excited and ready to guide you on this part of your Journey.

As you prepare to set off, imagine *Feeling Excited And Ready* for the opportunities ahead to learn more about yourself, and to experience continuous growth and self-improvement. Let's get started…

Your Ordinary World

"Before enlightenment chop wood, carry water.
After enlightenment chop wood, carry water."

—Zen Proverb

Your Transformative Journey begins the same as any heroic narrative, going about your daily tasks and activities in your Ordinary World. You have routines, commitments, and problem-solution cycles. You go through the motions, emotionally and mentally numb, or even worse, by continually thinking, feeling, communicating and behaving negatively.

On some level, you are aware that life has more to offer, or that you have the potential to be and do more. But the reality is you lack purpose, motivation, and/or direction. It's easier to go with the flow, to keep things status quo, and not risk the people and things you already have in your life.

The Sub-Life Scale

Below is the Sub-Life Scale, a continuum of different lifestyles. This is a sliding scale.

Read the descriptions of the lifestyles on the next page. Be aware that the journey through life is not usually a straight line. You can go through periods when everything seems to be on track, and going well. Then some event happens, which moves you up, or down, the scale.

The best way to use the Sub-Life Scale is to reflect on your current position by where you are 'living' the majority of your time. Then set a goal to where you want to live in the future.

Subsistent Lifestyle

You exist. You constantly struggle to survive, working to make ends meet, pay your bills, clothe yourself and your family, put food on your table, and keep a roof over your head. Your health may suffer, your energy and emotions will be low, and it is all you can do to get through each day. At the most extreme, you are reliant of the charity and support of others in order to survive.

Suburban Lifestyle

You live an average, "in-the-middle" lifestyle. You have enough income to meet your daily living requirements, put something by for your retirement, and occasionally upgrade your possessions or have a holiday somewhere away from where you live. You put other people before yourself and your needs, and tend to measure your level of success and happiness by theirs.

Substantial Lifestyle

You are financially independent, with residual or leveraged income from your passion-based ventures. Working is a choice, not a necessity. You have the freedom to live life exactly as you choose. You take care of your most important asset (you) first so that you can provide for the people you care about. You give back to the world by sharing your KESWIN™ in a variety of ways.

The Call to the Journey

"The Call to Adventure establishes the stakes of the game, and makes clear the hero's goal: to win the treasure or the lover, to get revenge or right a wrong, to achieve a dream, confront a challenge or change a life."

—Christopher Vogler, The Writer's Journey

One day, in your Ordinary World, something happens which causes you to take a good look at your life, and realise there is a significant problem or issue that you need to solve, and only you can solve it. You either choose to go on a Heroic Quest, or one is chosen for you by an external event, or you are issued a challenge that you accept.

The Call to the Journey often comes from deep within you, from your unconscious mind, the part of you that has been buried, suppressed and ignored for too long. It sends you a message in a dream, or through an unexpected emotional outburst, or the realisation that injustice is being done, or that there's more to life than you are currently experiencing.

It can also come from an unexpected event outside of your control, such as losing your job, having an accident, something being stolen from you, or surviving a disaster.

Calls to Adventure may also be presented by a Herald. They issue you a challenge, announce the approach of major change, or warn you of danger ahead if you keep on doing what you've always done. They may be a family member or friend, or a stranger who stirs feelings of unrest inside you, or an authority figure or expert who recognises that all is not well with you and you need to improve.

As the Hero in your Journey, it is up to you to answer the Call. If you choose to ignore it (often this is because fear gets the better of you), your refusal will be at your peril. Circumstances never ever improve on their own. If you are reluctant to answer the Call to the Journey, you risk something major forcing you into action.

Refusal of the Call

"For years I wished for my life to change, to have the opportunity to move to a new city, and work full-time on my dream. But I did nothing. And then... the Earthquake hit."

—Deb Donnell

In 2011, I became a Reluctant Hero, after refusing the Call to the Journey again and again. My daily life had become "Groundhog Day". I was marking time working in my parents' jewellery business, waiting for them to retire, so I could be free to work full-time on the vision I had in 2003.

A few months earlier, on 4 September 2010, the city where I live, Christchurch, New Zealand, had survived a 7.1 Magnitude earthquake, located 40 kilometres (25 miles) away. We lost a couple of buildings, and a lot more were partially damaged. Because the earthquake struck at 4:35 a.m., no life had been lost. As a city—and a region—we counted ourselves very lucky! We picked up bricks from our collapsed chimneys, swept away the broken china and glass inside our houses, and shovelled away the liquefaction (liquefied soil) from our yards and streets.

Life returned to normal, for most of us, by February 2011. And then, at 12:51 p.m. on February 22, a very shallow 6.3 magnitude earthquake struck on the outskirts of the city, centred in the Port of Lyttelton (it was 5 km/3.1 miles deep).

This earthquake was violent. It had a maximum vertical peak ground acceleration of 2.2 g-force. This meant that the energy released at the epicentre was 2.22 times the force of gravity.

It also had very violent vertical jolts as well as the more typical horizontal shaking. This is uncommon in an earthquake. This caused our buildings to bounce up and down as if they were jumping on a trampoline. It was extremely terrifying to experience such an unusual and violent earthquake!

Buildings collapsed all over the city, resulting in 185 deaths and thousands of injuries (of these, 164 survivors sustained serious crush injuries).

As with any mass trauma event, the majority of survivors have PTSD to varying degrees, and will carry this for the rest of our lives. There have been over 11,000 after shocks in the five year period that followed; a large percentage of them were felt by survivors. Add into that stress, the additional stress caused by ongoing insurance claims and bureaucratic red-tape, and the impact gets worse.

The violent earthquake has had a damaging impact on the psychological and physical development of young survivors, including those born in the year after the earthquake. Due to the PTSD resulting from being bounced into the air during the earthquake, and then experiencing the 11,000 plus aftershocks, they are extremely sensitive to unexpected noises, and physical or visual movement.

The high levels of stress hormones released over years has impacted on their neurological and biological development, adding to the stress of parents, their educators, and other caregivers.

My story is just one of over 450,000 unique stories told by the residents, visitors and rescuers who experienced the impact of the Christchurch Earthquake. The direction of our lives changed forever that day.

For me personally: before the Earthquake, I had ignored the Call to my Transformative Journey because of my fear of failure, my fear of success, my fear of disappointing the people I loved, and a whole raft of other fears relating to facing the unknown.

But on the afternoon of February 22, 2011, I emerged safely from the 150 year old broken building I had been working in. Inside our jewellery, our glass cabinets were shattered, their contents, including diamond rings and other jewellery, scattered on the floor. My parents' lifetime of hard work was destroyed in seconds.

Outside, the extent of destruction made the future very clear. Our city was destroyed. Our Ordinary World was gone. I could not ignore the Call to the Journey any longer.

Don't get me wrong. I know my refusal to answer the Call to the Journey earlier did not cause the Christchurch Earthquake. I'm not that important. No one is! But my life may have been different if I had.

We left the damaged city, walking through scenes reminiscent of being on the set of a Hollywood disaster movie. Only it was distressingly real. Over the next few hours, I checked on the status of the rest of my family and friends. Incredibly, all were safe and physically uninjured. I counted myself among the luckiest of survivors. The biggest personal impact (at that point) was the damage to my immediate family members' homes and to my parents' business.

I spent the first night at the safe-haven of a friend's house. There, I stood in front to the television, ready to flee if a big aftershock struck. I was in a state of shell-shock. Playing on the television was non-stop reporting on the search and rescue effort underway. Two multi-storey buildings had collapsed near the area I had fled from only hours before. The trained and volunteer rescuers were searching for survivors in the rubble, and in broken and burning buildings.

While I watched these nightmare images, I made three vows which have become my Quest to honour for the remainder of my life.

My Three Earthquake Vows

Vow 1: To the 185 Victims
I will stop refusing the Call to the Journey, and pursue my dreams to share my KESWIN™ and empower others to do the same.

Vow 2: To the Crush Injured Survivors
I will assist you, in some way, to adapt to the new circumstances of your life.

Vow 3: To the Courageous Rescuers
I will help you tell your story about your actions in the urban search, rescue and recovery effort to help our city during this dark moment in time.

In the years that have followed, I have done my best to honour my vows. The first one, to the victims who never made it home that day, honouring my vow is ongoing for the remainder of my Life's Journey.

The second one: in order to help the Crush Injured Survivors adapt to their changed lives, I voluntarily assisted the Canterbury Earthquake Survivors Trust for two years after the Earthquake. I did this by marketing their fundraising events, as well as donating author royalties of the books I published during those two years.

As for the third... although I did not know anyone in the rescue community at the time of February 2011. Towards the end of 2011, I was approached by Pete Seager, a New Zealand Response Team trained volunteer. He asked for my help to publish the organisation's Christchurch Earthquake story. This resulted in my co-authoring with him and publishing the 200 page book, *Responders: The New Zealand Volunteer Response Teams Christchurch Earthquake Deployments.*

My Quest, and the narratives relating to it, are shared in the content that I publish, the training material I present, and in other communications and interactions I have. My past experiences, especially in relation to the Christchurch Earthquake, are just some of the valuable treasure I have discovered on my Journeys.

You will discover valuable treasure on your Transformative Journeys too. I urge you not to be a reluctant Hero, like I was. Commit to the Journey now. Don't turn back before you even begin. Sure, the unknown that lies ahead may be terrifying. But do not let your fears stop you from leaving your Ordinary World and crossing the Threshold into an exciting and new Special World. You have already made a start, by reading this book. You may even have read others on the same topic before, but not heeded their Calls to Action.

And while I have given you a glimpse into facets of my Journey, I promise you that yours will be uniquely yours, and deeply personal to you. Please don't let a refusal to the Call to the Journey bring an event into your life that makes it even more personal, like I did.

Before 2011, I wanted to move to a new city. Instead, a new city is now moving towards me. The centre of Christchurch where I had grown up and spent most of my adult life working in, ended up being demolished because of the damage from the unusual vertical bouncing of the violent earthquake. Eight years later, it is only partially rebuilt.

I made this natural disaster personal, by choosing to document and publish books on the city's Transformative Journey. This was part of honouring the vows I made to the victims, crush injured survivors, and rescuers.

Remember my acronym for fear? *Feeling Excited And Ready*. It is much better than the more commonly shared meanings. Do not refuse the Call to the Journey. You do not want to be pushed by some devastating event into action, do you? Accept the Call now and prepare for your Transformative Journey.

Mentor (The Wise One)

"It's still magic even if you know how it's done."

—Terry Pratchett

I studied NLP and Neuro-Semantics to overcome my earthquake PTSD, my fears about answering the Call to the Journey, and to empower others to answer the Calls to their Transformative Journeys.

I first learned about NLP in the late 1990s. I was interested in developing skills to coach others. However, at that time, I refused the Call to that Journey.

In 2014, I met Dr. Alan Fayter, a Doctor of Clinical Hypnosis, IANLP Fellow Member Trainer and ISNS Master Trainer specialising in Neuro-Semantic Training, based on self-actualisation psychology. I helped him publish his book: *How to Chill Out: Earthquake Proof Strategies for Staying Calm in Any Crisis*.

Working on the book rekindled my interest in NLP. Over the next three years, Alan was my trainer and mentor as I worked towards getting my IANLP and ISNS NLP Master Practitioner certification.

At graduation, I shared with Alan and my fellow graduates that my newfound skill-set widens my range of KESWIN™. The result is I am able to provide effective training and mentoring to people wanting to go on similar Transformative Journeys to the ones I have been on.

Mentors are accessible through many forms of communication and interaction, such as in books and other published content, training courses, workshops, coaching, etc. They prepare you to enter the Special World of your Transformative Journey. They give advice, guidance, and even magical tools. They are also very good at giving Heroes—especially reluctant ones—swift kicks to get them going.

It is true that when the Hero is ready, the Mentor will appear. Just remember, the Mentor is only as valuable as the willingness of the Hero to accept the wisdom and resources being offered. So be open to welcoming in a Mentor, and excited about learning all you can learn from them.

Crossing into the Unknown

"The hero, having overcome fear, has decided to confront the problem and take action... is committed to the Journey and there's no turning back."

—Christopher Vogler, The Writer's Journey

As the Hero of Your Transformative Journey, this is the moment of decision, when you commit to change. It could be signing up for a workshop or training program, like I did, for personal improvement and/or to learn a new skill-set. It could be to change jobs, to adopt a new, healthier way of living, or to explore a new city. It could be to hire a coach, to reconnect with your creativity, or to start offering your KESWIN™ to others for a fee.

Your Journey is uniquely yours. Crossing into the Unknown, however, is the same for almost everyone. To enter the Special World you have chosen for your Quest, you need to pass through a gateway, or threshold of some kind, that takes you from your Ordinary World into a new, exciting one. You could be crossing a physical threshold. You might be moving through a marketing funnel, signing up for registration and entering the payment gateway. Or you may simply be making a mental decision to step through a symbolic door to start a new chapter in your life.

In the world of the movie, this is the turning point between Acts

One and Two. The Hero has decided to answer the Call to the Journey, to confront the challenge presented to them, and to step into the Special World where they believe the solution or the treasure they seek is hidden.

And while the unknown lies ahead, as the Hero of your Transformative Journey, you are resolved to continue on, no matter what, until you succeed in your Quest, or you die trying.

The Road of Trials, Friends & Foes

"A gem cannot be polished without friction, or a man perfected without trials."

—Lucius Annaeus Seneca

Stepping into the unknown provides you with plenty of opportunities, challenges, and tests. You learn new skills and the rules of the Special World, make new friends and allies, and even face encounters that strengthen your resolve and commitment to the Transformative Journey.

The battles and tests you face can be with external and internal enemies.

Externally:
Loved ones, friends, employers, or work colleagues not wanting you to change because they fear you'll leave them. People who refuse to be supportive because your growth and success makes them question their own journey and refusal to step out of their comfort zones.

Internally:
Emotional and mental skirmishes and conflicts that have the intention to keep you safe and protected. You sabotage your efforts, and retreat back to your bad habits and old ways of thinking and feeling. Even if you do attempt to change, you

suffer from imposter-syndrome, or struggle with a lack of self-worth, self-esteem, and self-confidence.

On a Transformative Journey, it is essential that you choose your friends and allies well. The best ones are supportive, nurturing, and encouraging. They ask if its okay to give constructed feedback. They don't tell you what to do or how to do it. Instead, they share the resources that have worked for them, stand at your side as your fight your enemies, and cheer you on in those moments when you have to fight alone.

Understand that with each trial faced, if you don't get the results you wanted, think of the failure as just feedback. Look for different angles, or better resources, so that you can get past any obstacles or roadblocks. Remind yourself that any detours are just different ways to get you to your chosen destination.

Because it is on the winding and steep Road of Trials that your KESWIN™ starts to really develop:

> ***K****nowledge is applied.*
> ***E****xperience grows.*
> ***S****kill-sets increase.*
> ***W****isdom is gained.*
> ***I****deas are brainstormed.*
> ***N****arratives are woven and told.*

Into the Dragon's Lair

"It is by going down into the abyss that we recover the treasures of life... The very cave you are afraid to enter turns out to be the source of what you are looking for."

—Joseph Campbell, Reflections on the Art of Living

There be Dragons Ahead... and plenty of them. On your Transformative Journey, dragons are the internal thoughts, feelings and conflicts that trip you up and block you, as well as critique and sabotage your efforts. They come in all shapes and sizes, and generally jump out and attack you when you least expect them to.

The thing about dragons is that they are the guardians of the treasure you seek. *Their highest intention is to protect you from being harmed by the external world.* How crazy is that! They want to keep you safe, and in doing so, end up keeping you wrapped in cotton wool.

So, how do you get past these dragons? After all, your Quest is to find the gems and other treasure that make up your unique talents and attributes, that have the potential to transform your life, and the lives of others.

The secret is to tame the dragons, to befriend them, to dance with them, and even share a good laugh with the silly creatures. To make them realise that you are the Hero in your

Transformative Journey, and you do not need their protection.

It is only by stepping into their lair, by facing them head on, and dancing with them, that you will recover the hopes and dreams of your past, and discover the valuable gems that you have created throughout your lifetime.

The dragons are hiding within you means that only you can fight them. However, it does help to have a non-judgemental ally at your side. When you have a good ally's respect, guidance and support, you have a very important resource for the most challenging part of your Transformative Journey... The Ordeal.

Dancing with Your Dragons

"I learned to accept and eventually even embrace my shadowy dragon-self. And just as in the legends, the dragon had a treasure horde to share with me."

—Rosemary Bane, Dancing in the Dragon's Den

In Western cultures, dragons are mostly portrayed as monsters to be feared. In Chinese mythology, they bring good fortune.

I have always loved dragons; from Puff the Magic dragon, to science-fiction author, Anne McCaffrey's world of Pern with majestic fire-breathing dragons, telepathically connected with their riders. I've collected many dragon treasures over the years and the first thing I learned to draw well was a cartoon dragon.

So, I had mixed feelings when, during our NS-NLP training, the metaphor of dragons was used for the fierce guardians of our shadowy darker side. But it also made it much easier for me to dance with these silly monsters undermining, limiting and even sabotaging my life as they hid inside my subconscious and unconscious minds!

On your Transformative Journey, this is the "Dark Moment of the Soul" (or The Ordeal) part of the story. This is where you discover the painful and dis-empowering reasons, intentions, meanings and processes behind your internal constructs of your experiences. It is where you analyse how you think and feel about your past communications and behaviours. You give yourself permission to accept all that has happened (the good, the bad, and the downright ugly), or change the narrative to a more positive one.

By acknowledging and accepting that you did the best you could do with the resources you had at the time, you can free up mental and emotional space to reflect on the positive aspects of events and experiences, and bring in new and empowering states, beliefs, understandings, and processes.

Note: If your dragons are emotionally or mentally debilitating, then please enlist the help of a qualified therapist.

Finding Your Treasure

"You are, at this moment, standing, right in the middle of your own 'acres of diamonds'."

—Earl Nightingale

Once you have tamed, accepted, and even befriended your well-intentioned dragons, you can then step deeper into the lair, and take possession of the valuable treasure you are seeking.

Treasure comes in all different forms, the value of which is unique to you. I refer to the treasure you find buried deep inside your unconscious mind as metaphorical diamonds formed from your KESWIN™.

As you step further into the dragon's lair, imagine your are stepping into the middle of your own "acres of diamonds."

Like natural diamonds, these have been created from your lifetime of experiences; the most valuable ones forming from the extreme pressure situations you've lived through.

Your KESWIN™ Diamonds lie deep inside your unconscious mind (the dragon's lair). It is up to you, the Hero of your story, to bring these rough gems back with you to the Ordinary World, where you will assess which are the most valuable, and then cut and polish them for your benefit, and also to share with others.

So, look around the cave with awareness.

Appreciate all the **K**nowledge, **E**xperiences, **S**kill-sets, **W**isdom, **I**deas, and **N**arratives you have gained throughout your life.

Access a sense of awe as you analyse the multitude of gems spread around you.

Appropriate and select the diamonds most relevant to your Quest on this Transformative Journey.

Accept that you cannot carry them all back with you this time.

Acknowledge that you can make your Transformative Journeys again... and again... and again...

And when you are ready, it's time to start heading back to the Ordinary World that is waiting for you to return with your unique and valuable treasure.

Heading Back to Reality

"Every hero must return home. Starks to Winterfell. Harry to Privet Drive. Luke Skywalker to Tattoine. Katniss to District Twelve. The fun is in seeing how they return."

—Pierce Brown, Author

After you have selected and packed the treasure you find deep in your unconscious mind, you realise that you have to return to the Ordinary World, and all the real life problems and issues it contains.

On the road back, if you haven't reconciled or tamed all of your dragons, you may still have some of them chase you through the valleys of your subconscious mind.

Make sure any decisions for change aren't too overwhelming. Don't let self-doubts sabotage your efforts. Ensure that you stay focused on the road back to consciousness, and travel it swiftly.

There may be temptations and distractions to test your resolve; it's up to you to stay committed to the Quest, and not to give up your hard-won rewards to shapeshifters, insincere friends, or vengeful enemies.

There is danger in sharing your newly discovered, or rediscovered, **K**nowledge, **E**xperiences, **S**kill-sets or **W**isdom too soon, before you have had a chance to cut and polish your valuable gems.

Don't give away **I**deas too easily. Don't be too quick to share your **N**arratives. Take time to assess, plan and strategize how to best deliver your KESWIN™ Diamonds to prospective audiences or clients.

The key here lies in making the decision to return to the Ordinary World, and to commit to making a difference to others by sharing the treasure you have found on your Transformative Journey.

Emerging as the New You

"I believe that God has put gifts and talents and ability on the inside of every one of us. When you develop that and you believe in yourself and you believe that you're a person of influence and a person of purpose, I believe you can rise up out of any situation."

—Joel Osteen

A Transformative Journey is one where you travel deep into your heart, soul, and mind. You reflect on your present and make peace with your past. You tame your dragons, reconstruct the negative, strengthen the positive, and envision better ways of thinking, feeling, behaving and communicating in the future.

The overview of the Transformative Journey shared here is based on the Hero's Journey. I've drawn on my own KESWIN™, which includes the study and training I've undertaken in self-actualisation psychology (Neuro-Semantics and Neuro Linguistics Programming).

When you go on a Transformative Journey to discover the gifts, talents and abilities—your KESWIN™ Diamonds—hidden in the dragon's lair, the old 'You' will be no more. Your old beliefs, values, habits, feelings, behaviours, and even desires will disappear.

You are the Hero in your story. You visit the Special World hidden within you.

When you emerge into the Ordinary World, the person you were when you left is no longer.

You shed your old ways. You view daily interactions and activities with newfound excitement and curiosity. Your values and beliefs align with your goals and actions. You have new purpose and meaning to your life.

Now you are ready to fully return to the Ordinary World as the new you.

Sharing Your KESWIN™

"Like me, Deb does not want you to die with a book still inside you."

—Dan Poynter (1938-2015), Self-Publishing Pioneer

Like many Heroes who have returned from their Transformative Journeys, you may find yourself gravitating more and more towards activities that align with your new purpose. You focus on what is meaningful to you, on what you are passionate about, and what makes your heart sing.

And because your heart is singing, you will want to share your passion with others through some form of communication. You may want to inform, educate, or entertain via writing, speaking, publishing, or selling your KESWIN™ Diamonds. This may be something you have considered, but are unsure of how to get started.

When I was ten years old, I decided I would be an author, writing books that would entertain, inspire and empower my readers. But it wasn't until 2003 that I got the courage to self-publish my first book, *Trails to Treasure: A Collection of Short Stories*.

Despite having worked for two years in the UK publishing industry in the early 1990s, I wasn't sure how to do this. So I turned to "Mr Publishing" Dan Poynter's book, *The Self-Publishing Manual.* Dan was the world's leading expert on how to write, print, and sell your own book. He became my mentor.

In 2007, I got to meet him in person when he came to Christchurch, New Zealand, to run a self-publishing workshop. I was one of four attendees. His belief in the concept I was working on gave me confidence to pursue my dream and become a local best-selling author and independent publisher.

Dan was also a pioneer of marketing on the Internet, which is a crucial part of building an authoritative brand. In 2008, I decided to learn more about online marketing from another US based mentor, Ann Sieg. This took me to a new Special World, where I gained the skills and confidence to set up my first training academy with partners based in the US and UK. We trained people to set up an online business and share what makes their heart sing through content marketing.

In October 2009, Dan Poynter returned to Christchurch to speak to our local National Speakers Association branch. Before he arrived, I emailed him, and asked him if he'd let me interview him after the talk. He very generously agreed, and later on left a comment on my blog in November 2009 (see the quote at the start of this chapter). I was so excited to have him post this challenge to me, along with:

> *"Getting together with Deb was a privilege and a pleasure. She was a major highlight to my trip to Christchurch."*

The interview is available to listen to at KESWIN™ Academy.

Dan Poynter supported and endorsed my dream. In 2015, I was sad to learn he had died, as were all of the authors, skydivers, and professional speakers around the world who he had inspired and mentored.

His last update of *The Self-Publishing Manual* claimed to have launched a million+ books. His passing has meant the baton has been handed onto me, and numerous others, to ensure that *"you do not die with your book still inside of you."*

However, I'm not just wanting to make sure you do not die with a book still inside of you. I want to empower you to discover, mine, cut, polish, and share your valuable KESWIN™ Diamonds through building a passion-based business.

This is so easy and affordable to achieve with the advances of technology. However, for many people born in the Gen-X and Baby Boomer eras, technology is a threat to every facet of our lives. Mastering and controlling it is an ongoing challenge, as is achieving the success we desire in order to lead successful and substantial lives.

Many Gen-X and Baby Boomers face self-esteem and self-confidence issues now more than at any other time of their lives. With the current conversations in the media and online, it's not just women left questioning our upbringing, our values, our beliefs, our experiences, the popular stories, movies and TV shows, and actions of our idols and heroes from our past.

What was once deemed "acceptable" behav-iour is no longer acceptable or politically correct. In some instances, this has led to criminal investigations and convictions.

This is not necessarily a bad thing, especially where a person has used their position of authority or celebrity status to justify their criminal actions to another person. However, these changes to society's values, beliefs, and standards do have an impact on our internal maps and landscapes about the "reality" of the external world.

New technology which is easily adopted by the younger generations is ripping the fabric of the world that Gen-Xers and Baby Boomers were raised in. And, just as with any process that disrupts the past norms, the pendulum of change is swinging rapidly to the opposite extreme, and in many cases is being more polarising than it is equalising. My hope is that it will eventually settle to a balanced and fair new normal.

I believe that the growing trend towards personal development is a major part of the Transformative Journey the world is on.

If the message in this book has resonated with you in any way, inspired you, or called you to seek treasure hidden inside you, then please connect with me online (see last page).

I also urge you to continue this Journey on your own, by studying a wide range of content on personal development and other relevant topics from the world's leading thought leaders and experts.

Discover your KESWIN™, release your trapped Diamonds, and live your life with your heart singing!

About KESWIN™ Academy

Our Mission

To guide You to become an authentic, empowered, confident, and valuable thought leader who engages, inspires, and empowers your followers by sharing your KESWIN™ in your niche market.

KESWIN™ Academy is a small online community of like-minded individuals, with similar quests… to be the Hero in their Transformative Journeys.

It is a partnership between KESWIN™ Publishing Ltd and Writing Diamonds Ltd. Founded by Deb Donnell, NS-NLP Master Practitioner, Author and Entrepreneur.

A maximum of 100 members are personally guided by Deb through a series of Trans-formative Journeys, to help them identify what makes their heart sing. Many go on to share their unique and valuable talents and attributes through building personal and/or business brands.

We are based in New Zealand, but are accessible via the Internet from wherever you are. If you would like to know how to join us, or just get more info, please visit https://Keswin.Academy.

Testimonials

These testimonials are from charter members of Writing Diamonds Academy, the beta version of KESWIN™ Academy. The leadership team has not changed... only the name and some facets of the training content have been revised, upgraded or added. The missing ingredient in the beta version was the focus on personal development. KESWIN™ Academy (Version 2.0) addresses this oversight by making personal development the foundation of all training modules.

"This is different to most typical training programs where you buy and listen to the training. The difference is that learning and doing is incorporated into the program. There is a lot of interaction between members and trainers, and you can ask questions. The people behind it have a genuine go-getter attitude. The material is never stale—it's always cutting edge, and that's fantastic. I feel pretty lucky to have been a part of Writing Diamonds Academy. It's not easy—it takes work, but it's a great experience. I certainly recommend it to people looking to build an authoritative online presence."
—Dennis Roberts, USA

"I've learned about effective market research tools, business organization skills, building blogs, writing articles, copyright information, social networks and their use, strategies for successful soft marketing, a few technical skills, how to set up a marketing funnel online, and the list goes on. And I've had a really good time doing it! Being part of a small group provides an awesome learning environment where we can all find help, and help others too. We occasionally just socialize and have fun too. I've made some awesome friendships."
—Barb Schacher, USA

"Most products or coaches assume you know the basics of online marketing and technical terminology, and have technical skills. I know in the end we are each responsible for what we want to create. However, I don't feel like I'm all alone. The short videos and interactive training events are very helpful. There is always someone available to help with an issue. I'm very grateful to have a safe place to build my income generating business. It makes the journey so much more enjoyable and easier."
—HS, USA *(Name withheld at member's request)*

"Writing Diamonds Academy has made me really excited about writing! I just needed someone to get me in the habit and doing it. Now I feel like I am on a roll. The presentation on writing our "About Me" page was outstanding and helped me so much!"
—Nicole Thomas, USA

"There is too much information on the Internet about marketing, which makes you confused about exactly where to start. With Writing Diamonds Academy, you receive precise instructions in an easy to follow format. Being part of a group offers support and mentorship that enables everyone to work together and feel part of a team, while building their own business. The focus on writing helps make writing easier."
—Tania Wilder, Australia

"Writing Diamonds Academy is a safe environment, where I feel I can be myself and ask questions, or offer my ideas. I have a support system of honest, genuine, like-minded people from around the world, who don't think I'm crazy or stupid to try something different. The training is broken down into small parts, so I can tackle a bit at a time. I have learned both fundamental techniques, and others that I would call advanced. Material is up-to-date and presented in an understandable format. It is so great to have people helping people succeed."
—Kris Newland, USA

"Writing challenges me. I love the videos—I can stop them and move at my own pace, and it helps me get a better understanding. The people are great! I am forming solid relationships, and can get help from my peers as well as the trainers. I have learned a lot about online marketing."
—Heather Hansen, Canada

"The training in Writing Diamonds Academy is a lot more dialogue than presentation. It has helped me transition from learning mode to doing mode. The modules in writing, market research, blogging and business management have been both instructional and hands-on practice. Even though I'm building my own business, I'm not doing it alone, as I'm part of a community of people with similar goals. I find plenty of encouragement, peer support, and camaraderie within the network. The result-oriented leaders have high ethical standards, are knowledgeable, current, even cutting edge, and most of all, accessible."
—Bob Young, USA

"Since joining Writing Diamonds Academy, I've accomplished more and written more than I did before. It's a supportive environment, where I have peers helping me gauge where I am in the training. I receive help when I need it, and we can bounce ideas off each other. The knowledgeable trainers and coaches guide us through the Internet business maze and demonstrate that they actually do care about us achieving our goals."
—Felicia Waren, USA

"Before I joined, I was just watching and listening to other online marketing training programs with no real plan. Isn't that Crazy? If I hadn't joined Writing Diamonds Academy, and had the opportunity to learn with others, I would have hung up my dream by now. The trainers' efforts to make our writing skills exceptional, and adapt the training to our needs is outstanding. It's also powerful having made new friends with people from all over the world, and that they are willing to step up and help me without question."
—Marshall Joyce, USA

"Writing Diamonds Academy provides low-cost, state-of-the-art training. I have a road map to follow, people to connect with, and trainers who are genuinely there for us. They give 120% to ensure we all succeed. They are helping us create businesses that are genuine and legitimate, with no hype or in your face tactics. This is so different to anything I've experienced before."
—Claire Newell, New Zealand

"I was having trouble writing content for my blog and understanding social Internet marketing. Writing Diamonds Academy helped me build up my confidence. It is a safe place to ask questions, get help, and immediately apply what we are learning. I have fun building lasting relationships with other members. It's value exceeds the affordable price I pay as a member."
—Lanette Passarelli, USA

"Writing Diamonds Academy provides a fresh approach to learning online. The mentors and members are real people you can talk to and build lasting relationships with. The training is professional and easy to follow. The workshops are fun and interactive. You can get your questions answered immediately, which is especially valuable if you have a problem you can't work out on your own."
—Corinne Floyd, Canada

"Deb has helped me improve my writing skills tremendously. Now, I not only have the confidence to sit and write, but I have the basic ability to communicate intelligibly while delivering some real value. This was a skill that was well beyond me prior to becoming a member."
—Tom Renfro, USA

"I am grateful that Deb took the time to show me how to write diamonds. I do believe within all of us there are diamonds that need to be put down on paper. When they are inside of us, nobody sees or hears them. And just to think I almost didn't take this course! What a loss I would have experienced. As I write every day I feel a sense of who I am and who I might become. Keep those diamonds coming; there are many of us who need them."
—Greg Gust, USA

The following testimonials are from New Zealand based clients who have attended offline workshops run by Deb Donnell and then worked directly with her to write, edit, and publish their non-fiction books that share their KESWIN™.

"Deb provides good, practical information in her workshops, especially relating to the legal requirements and other aspects of publishing."
—Jane Cowan-Harris
Author of 10 Secrets to Creating a Healthy Home-Based Office

"Working with Deb gave me a real understanding of the factors involved to publish a book. I never would have completed my project without her."
—David Clarkson
Author of Dare to Deliver: The Dynamic Guide to Public Speaking

"It's awesome having Deb work with me to produce a real book! She delivers clear instructions and gives practical support in a friendly and approachable manner."
—Dr Alan Fayter
Author of How to Chill Out: Earthquake Proof Strategies for Staying Calm in Any Crisis

About Deb Donnell

Author, Publisher
FOUNDER: KESWIN™ Academy
GIA Diamonds Graduate
NS-NLP Master Practitioner

Thanks for taking the time to read this book, which is part of the journey I started in 2003. This was when I first clarified what makes my heart sing. Although I had known this since 1979, I had buried during my teens and twenties, because I was scared that others would think it was the wrong path for me to travel. It wasn't until I was about to turn 40 that I actually begin believing in myself enough to really pursue my heart's desire… and then…

In February 2011, a violent earthquake struck my city, and buried my dreams underneath the rubble.

Over the next 7 years I went on a number of Quests to develop the KESWIN™ System and fill in some gaps in my own skill-sets. This included:

- independently publishing several best-selling books;
- completing my Gemological Institute of America (GIA) Diamonds—this means I can identify, grade and value natural diamonds as well as people's metaphorical ones; and
- studying Neuro-Semantics and NLP (Neuro Linguistics Programming) to deal with my earthquake trauma. I learned how to run my own brain, and guide others to do the same.

The Christchurch Earthquake tried to take my dreams from me. Instead, I made the decision to "dig through the rubble" and rebuild what I had lost. This included revising and rebranding the online business training academy I had co-founded in 2008.

It is now my pleasure to introduce you to KESWIN™ Academy. It is an exclusive online community (up to 100 members) where I mentor people through the Transformative Journey. As a member, you will leverage off my KESWIN™ to identify yours, discover what makes your heart sing, and how you can live an authentic life following your passion.

If you'd like to find out if we're a good fit for each other, and have a no-obligation personal tour of KESWIN™ Academy, please set up a time to chat by completing the form at: https://keswin.academy/book-tour/

Thank you for reading my book. If you enjoyed it, I'd appreciate if you could please take a moment to leave me a review at your favourite retailer.

And remember… *Don't die with your KESWIN™ trapped inside!*

Deb Donnell

Next in the YOU Series

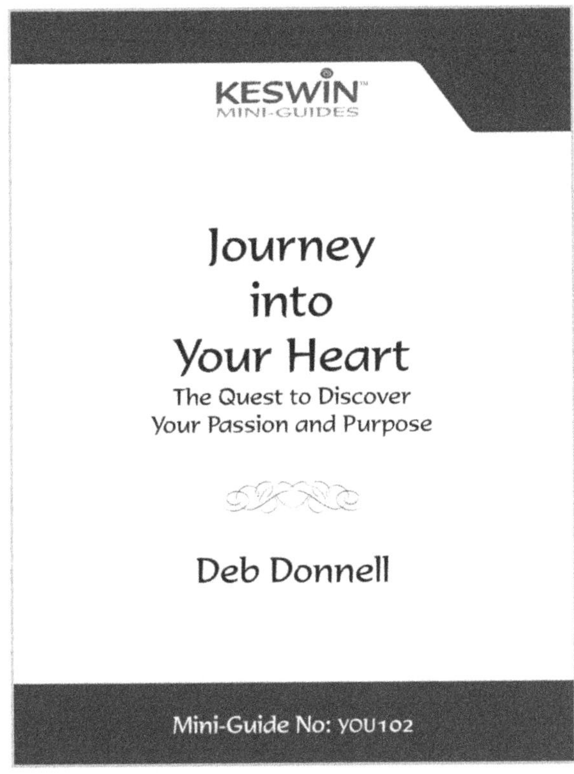

YOU102: Journey into Your Heart - The Quest to Discover Your Passion and Purpose focuses on helping you to identify your values, meaning, and purpose, and aligning them with your passion. Once you have clarity about what makes your heart sing, you can set achievable goals to focus on.

Available from our website or your favourite online retailer.

Connect with Deb Donnell

You can message me via my personal or business websites, or via social networks.

Visit my website: https://DebDonnell.info

Follow me on:

Facebook: https://www.facebook.com/DebDonnellAuthor

Twitter: https://twitter.com/debdonnell

LinkedIn: https://nz.linkedin.com/in/debdonnell

Google+: https://plus.google.com/+DebDonnell

Goodreads: https://www.goodreads.com/author/show/4180664.Deb_Donnell

Review this book online at the store from where you bought it.

More information about KESWIN™ Academy, or to book a tour and a no-obligation chat: https://keswin.academy

www.ingramcontent.com/pod-product-compliance
Ingram Content Group UK Ltd.
Pitfield, Milton Keynes, MK11 3LW, UK
UKHW020238250726
13967UKWH00001B/434

9 780958 278072